AIR FORCE

Civilian to AIRMAN

by Meish Goldish

Consultant: Fred Pushies
U.S. SOF Adviser

BEARPORT
PUBLISHING

New York, New York

Credits

Cover and Title Page, © U.S. Air Force/Tech. Sgt, Scott T. Sturkol and U.S. Air Force/Senior Airman Steven R. Doty; 4, © U.S. Air Force photo/Benjamin Faske; 5L, © U.S. Air Force photo/Alan Boedeker; 5R, © U.S. Air Force photo/Consolidated News Photos/Newscom; 6T, Courtesy of Keetra Baker; 6B, © U.S. Air Force photo/ Master Sgt. Cecilio Ricardo; 7, © U.S. Air Force photo/Master Sgt. Cecilio Ricardo; 8T, © U.S. Air Force photo/ Robbin Cresswell; 8B, © U.S. Air Force photo/Robbin Cresswell; 9T, © U.S. Air Force photo/Alan Boedeker; 9B, © U.S. Air Force photo/Robbin Cresswell; 10, © U.S. Air Force photo/Senior Airman Christopher Griffin; 11L, © U.S. Air Force photo/Alan Boedeker; 11R, © U.S. Air Force photo/Alan Boedeker; 12, © U.S. Air Force photo/ Robbin Cresswell; 13T, © David Chappell Photography; 13B, © AP Images/Eric Gay; 14, © U.S. Air Force photo/ Tech. Sgt. Cecilio Ricardo Jr.; 15L, © U.S. Air Force photo/Tech. Sgt. Beth Holliker; 15R, © U.S. Air Force photo/ Nan Wylie; 16, © U.S. Air Force photo/Danny Meyer; 17, © U.S. Air Force photo/Senior Airman Tim Bazar; 18, © U.S. Air Force photo/Staff Sgt. Jason Lake; 19, © U.S. Air Force photo/Master Sgt. Scott Moorman; 20-21, © Purestock/StockTrek/SuperStock; 22A, © DOD photo by Cherie Cullen; 22B, © AP Images/David Zalubowski; 22C, © brt photo/Alamy; 22D, © U.S. Air Force photo/Staff Sgt. Jason Lake; 22E, © Purestock/StockTrek/ SuperStock.

Publisher: Kenn Goin
Senior Editor: Lisa Wiseman
Creative Director: Spencer Brinker
Design: Debrah Kaiser
Photo Researcher: James O'Connor

Library of Congress Cataloging-in-Publication Data

Goldish, Meish.
  Air Force : civilian to airman / by Meish Goldish ; consultant, Fred Pushies.
     p. cm. — (Becoming a soldier)
  Includes bibliographical references and index.
  ISBN-13: 978-1-936088-10-2 (library binding)
  ISBN-10: 1-936088-10-X (library binding)
  1. United States. Air Force—Juvenile literature. I. Title.
  UG633.G614 2011
  358.400973—dc22
                         2010004151

For more information, write to Bearport Publishing Company, Inc., 101 Fifth Avenue, Suite 6R, New York, New York 10003. Printed in the United States of America in North Mankato, Minnesota.

122010
120810CGC

10 9 8 7 6 5 4 3 2

Contents

Getting Tough

A long line of **trainees** hung in midair from the monkey bars. They held tightly to the metal rungs above their heads. Slowly, they pulled themselves forward along the bars. Though they were exhausted and their hands burned, they didn't dare let go. One slip and they would fall into the muddy pit below— and have to start all over again.

Trainees in the air force take part in many military exercises that help prepare them mentally and physically for war.

This **military** exercise was just one of many demanding tests that trainees such as Christopher Platte had to go through to become **airmen** in the U.S. Air Force. Yet for Christopher, all the effort was worth it. By joining the air force, he had followed in the footsteps of both his grandfather and great-uncle. They had been U.S. pilots during World War II (1939–1945). They inspired him to work hard and to do his best.

Christopher's grandfather and great-uncle were part of the Tuskegee Airmen—the first African American pilots in the U.S. military.

The air force is the branch of the **armed forces** responsible for military operations in the air.

At his airman graduation ceremony in December 2009, Christopher (right) watched his great-uncle (left) sign a wall dedicated to the Tuskegee Airmen.

Welcome to Lackland

It took a lot of hard work for Christopher to become an airman. Like all men and women who have **enlisted** in the air force, he spent a grueling eight and a half weeks going through basic military training, or BMT, at Lackland Air Force Base in Texas. Here, trainees spend long hours learning tough **combat** and survival skills as well as air force history and values.

Lackland Air Force Base, located in San Antonio, Texas, is nicknamed "The Gateway to the Air Force" because all enlisted men and women get their basic training there.

Before basic training begins, male trainees must get very short haircuts or shave their heads, while females have to make sure their hair is not longer than the collars of their uniforms.

New arrivals at the base are first divided into groups called **flights**. Each flight has about 45 members and is led by a military training **instructor**, or MTI. His or her job is to teach the former **civilians** all about military life. After trainees are put into flights, they are assigned **dormitories** and receive their uniforms. Now the hard work begins.

An MTI yells out orders to his flight.

During BMT, all enlisted men and women refer to themselves as "trainees." For example, Christopher Platte would address his MTI with "Sir, Trainee Platte reports as ordered."

A Long, Hard Day

During BMT, the day begins early—at 4:45 AM. With only 15 minutes to get dressed, trainees rush to prepare for the difficult day ahead of them. On some days, they start with strength training. On others, they begin with an hourlong run. The MTIs follow the flight, screaming at the trainees to stay together. Even when their legs begin to ache, trainees aren't allowed to rest.

Trainees eat a healthy breakfast after physical training.

During BMT, trainees work hard to get into top physical shape.

Besides preparing themselves physically during the first five weeks of BMT, trainees also learn teamwork, **discipline**, fighting techniques, first aid, and all the skills they need to become successful airmen. For example, they spend hours practicing **drills** such as marching together and saluting. They repeat these exercises over and over, until they can hardly stand up.

During this time, trainees are also taught to assemble, clean, and shoot their M16 rifles. Though their fingers might be sore, they work until they get the process right. MTIs can be heard barking orders and commands at their flights until the day finally ends at 9:00 PM.

Trainees take aim during weapons practice.

MTIs are known for being tough. They set high standards and goals for the trainees. They're constantly yelling commands and will punish anyone who doesn't follow orders or work as a team with the flight. For example, if a trainee makes a mistake, the instructor may have him or her do push-ups.

Each trainee learns how to assemble, shoot, and clean a rifle.

Surviving the BEAST

The sixth week of BMT is the hardest. During this time, trainees face the BEAST—or Basic **Expeditionary** Airman Skills Training. The purpose of the exercise is for trainees to feel as if they are really in combat.

Trainees must work together to survive on the battlefield.

During BEAST week, dummies are used to portray the enemy. Sometimes fellow airmen are used as well.

During BEAST week, all flights move from their dormitories to a large battlefield on the base, where they set up tents. For the next few days, trainees take part in a fake war, where attacks can come at any time—day or night. It's not uncommon to see sweaty trainees crawling across the hard ground on their bellies, searching for the enemy. As they make their way through the dirt, they watch for bombs disguised as soda cans. One mistake and a trainee can be declared "dead."

A trainee searching for the enemy during BEAST week.

A female trainee practices her fighting skills during BEAST week.

Ready to Graduate

After the trainees complete BEAST week, they are almost done with BMT. During their final weeks, they must pass a fitness test, which includes a timed run, plus push-ups and sit-ups. Trainees also take two written exams on their knowledge of the air force. Those who pass everything are set to graduate. Those who fail may need to repeat part of basic training.

A trainee doing push-ups

In order to pass the fitness test, men must finish a 1.5-mile (2.4-km) run in less than 11 minutes, 57 seconds, and women need to complete the run in less than 13 minutes, 56 seconds. Also, men must complete 45 push-ups and 50 sit-ups, each within 1 minute. Women must do 27 push-ups and 50 sit-ups, each within 1 minute as well.

At BMT graduation, trainees become airmen. They are each awarded the Airman's Coin to symbolize their transformation from trainees to airmen. Their air force careers have not ended, however. In fact, they are just beginning.

Airmen each receive the Airman's Coin, a symbol of their achievements during BMT.

A graduation ceremony at Lackland

Job Choices

What happens after BMT? An airman is now ready to train for a job in the air force. The type of job an airman chooses depends on his or her interests and abilities.

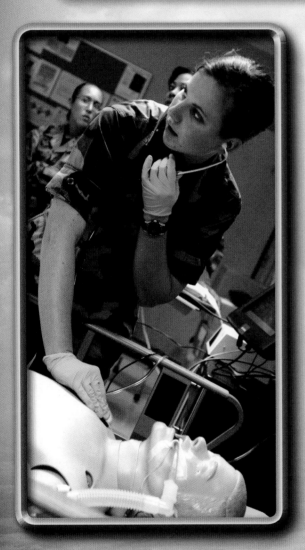

Some airmen go through medical technical training.

After choosing a job, most airmen are trained at one of five air force bases around the country: Lackland, Goodfellow, or Sheppard in Texas; Keesler in Mississippi; or Vandenberg in California. Job training can last anywhere from a few weeks to a full year, depending on the type of work an airman is training for.

● **Air Force Training Locations**

There are nearly 200 different jobs available to airmen. For example, an airman might become an airplane **mechanic** who fixes planes, or a weather **analyst** who studies weather conditions for flying. Airmen do not become pilots, however. Pilots join the air force in a completely different way.

Airmen do not fly planes. Instead, their jobs let them lend support to the pilots and the aircraft. This airman is a mechanic preparing the plane for a training mission.

An air force weather analyst (left) discusses the weather conditions with an air force pilot (right).

Inside the Academy

Air force pilots do not start out as trainees at Lackland. Instead, many future fliers begin their careers at the Air Force **Academy** in Colorado, a four-year military college. Students enter as **cadets** and graduate as **officers**. Only officers can go on to become air force pilots.

When they start the academy, cadets go through basic military training. Like trainees, they learn combat skills and study air force history and values.

At the academy, cadets take many military and science courses. They learn to fly simple planes such as **motor gliders** and the Cessna T-41. Cadets who pass their flying tests go on to advanced flight instruction after graduating from the academy.

The Air Force Academy has both male and female cadets who can become officers as well as pilots. However, it wasn't until 1994 that U.S. law allowed women to fly in combat.

A female cadet (right) reviews the instrument panel on a plane.

Other Ways to Fly

Going to the academy is just one way to become an air force officer. Another way is to join the Reserve Officers' Training Corps, also known as ROTC. This is a military program offered at many colleges. ROTC students receive air force training and flight instruction while getting a college degree. They graduate as officers who can then go on to become pilots.

ROTC students go through intense physical training. The program produces a large number of air force officers who go on to become pilots.

ROTC is available at about 150 colleges and universities around the country. Students take regular college courses in addition to their military training. ROTC pays for a portion of the students' college costs.

Still another way to become a pilot is through Officer Training School at Maxwell Air Force Base in Alabama. There, college graduates take a tough 12-week training course. They are taught flying, combat, and leadership skills. They graduate as officers who can then take more training to become air force pilots.

Trainees at Officer Training School at Maxwell Air Force Base learning self-defense moves

Serving the Nation

Today, more than 300,000 men and women serve in the U.S. Air Force. Most have jobs on the ground. Some fly the planes. Yet all share a common purpose: to protect the United States from enemy threats in the air.

The air force protects the skies to keep the United States safe.

In recent years, the dangers of war and **terrorism** have spread around the world. So members of the air force now serve in more places than ever before, including Iraq and Afghanistan. They proudly live by the air force's core **values**: "**Integrity** first. Service before self. Excellence in all we do."

Enlisted airmen serve in the air force for at least 4 years. Officers who become pilots serve at least 10 years. An airman or officer can also make the air force a lifetime career.

Preparing for the Air Force

If you are interested in joining the air force in the future, you can start preparing now by doing well in school, keeping your body in top physical shape, and being a responsible person. According to the U.S. government, the following rules apply:

To Enter as an Enlisted Person

★ Must be between 17 and 28 years old

★ Must have a high school diploma or a general **equivalency** diploma (GED)

★ Must pass a skills test and a physical exam

To Enter the Air Force Academy

★ Must be between 17 and 22 years old

★ Must be a high school graduate with high grades; most academy students finished in the top quarter of their high school class.

★ Must be nominated by a member of the U.S. Congress

★ Must pass a physical fitness test that includes running and push-ups

To Enter ROTC

★ Must be enrolled in a college or university

★ Must pass a physical fitness test that includes running and push-ups

To Enter Officer Training School

★ Must be a college graduate

★ Must be between 18 and 34 years old

★ Must pass a physical fitness test that includes running and push-ups

academy (uh-KAD-uh-mee) a school that teaches special subjects

airmen (AIR-men) the first rank for enlisted men and women after completing air force basic training

analyst (AN-uh-list) a person who studies something carefully in order to understand it

armed forces (ARMD FORSS-iz) the military groups a country uses to protect itself; in the United States these are the Army, the Navy, the Air Force, the Marines, and the Coast Guard

cadets (kuh-DETS) students training for the armed forces at a military school

civilians (si-VIL-yuhnz) people who are not members of the armed forces

combat (KOM-bat) fighting between people or armies

discipline (DISS-uh-plin) control over the way a person or others behave

dormitories (DOR-muh-*tor*-eez) buildings with rooms to sleep in

drills (DRILZ) military training exercises, such as handling a weapon, that are practiced over and over

enlisted (en-LIST-id) joined a branch of the armed forces

equivalency (i-KWIV-uh-luhn-see) being equal in value or significance

expeditionary (*ek*-spuh-DISH-uh-*ner*-ee) a kind of armed force that is organized to accomplish a specific objective in a foreign country

flights (FLITES) groups of air force trainees who are going through basic training

instructor (in-STRUHKT-uhr) a teacher

integrity (in-TEG-ruh-tee) the quality of being honest and sincere

mechanic (muh-KAN-ik) someone who is skilled at using or fixing a machine

military (MIL-uh-*ter*-ee) having to do with soldiers or war

motor gliders (MOH-tur GLYE-durz) airplanes that can be flown with or without engine power

officers (AWF-uh-surz) people in the military who are in charge of others

terrorism (TER-ur-iz-uhm) the use of threats and violence to scare and control other people

trainees (tray-NEEZ) people who are being taught particular work skills

values (VAL-yooz) a person's beliefs and ideas about what is important

Index

Bibliography

Camelo, Wilson. *The U.S. Air Force and Military Careers.* Berkeley Heights, NJ: Enslow (2006).

Holden, Henry M. *To Be a U.S. Air Force Pilot.* Osceola, WI: Zenith Press (2004).

Read More

Hopkins, Ellen. *United States Air Force.* Chicago: Heinemann Library (2004).

Zobel, Derek. *United States Air Force.* Minneapolis, MN: Bellwether (2008).

Learn More Online

To learn more about the U.S. Air Force, visit
www.bearportpublishing.com/BecomingaSoldier

About the Author

Meish Goldish has written more than 200 books for children. He lives in Brooklyn, New York.